AF265291

Beyond Conscious Thought

Inspirational Messages
Volume II

Opening to Spirit Series

N. J. Fenttiman

Copyright © N.J. Fenttiman, 2020
Published: 2020 by
The Book Reality Experience

ISBN: 978-0-6489404-3-2 - Paperback Edition
ISBN: 978-0-6489404-2-5 - Ebook Edition

All rights reserved.

The right of N.J. Fenttiman to be identified as the author of this Work has been asserted by her in accordance with sections 77 and 78 of the Copyright, Designs and Patents Act 1988.

The information contained in this book is of a general nature and should not be regarded as legal advice or relied on for assistance in any particular circumstance or emergency situation.

The Publisher and author jointly or singularly, accept no responsibility or liability for any damage, loss or expense incurred as a result of the reliance on information contained in this book.

Any third party views or recommendations included in this book do not reflect the views of the Publisher, or indicate its commitment to a particular course of action.

No part of this publication may be reproduced, stored in a retrieval system, copied in any form or by any means, electronic, mechanical, photocopying, recording or otherwise transmitted without written permission from the publisher. You must not circulate this book in any format.

Cover design Luke Buxton | www.lukebuxton.com
From an original drawing by N.J. Fenttiman adapted by Lisa Townsend

To Matthew

Introduction

In recent decades there has been a renewed, almost urgent interest in the search for meaning and guidance in one's life and in the lives of many others. The 'church' not seeming to satisfy this desire left many, myself included, with a sense or a need to find a knowing, an understanding and a connectedness that would fill the void and heal the spirit.

Hello! I am Norma. I had for many years known that there was 'more' about me than I could logically perceive. My Mother was an 'intuitive' and often sensed death or illness about a person. She, therefore, tried to shield me from developing my intuition.

It was in 1994 (aged 51), when I enrolled in a Bachelor of Arts degree in English Studies, that I discovered a number of my colleagues had intuitive/psychic abilities. There were two mediums and a healer in my class.

"Why aren't you working?" I was asked "Me, how?" And so with Gwen and Marg's guidance and meditation, the process began.

I began to write - "Let the words flow, without conscious control." Many a page went into the bin. Finally, I stepped aside and trusted. And in that trust, so much more of my life and experiences made sense.

I was writing, I thought, for myself. Some days asking

for assistance and guidance, with life's difficulties and others for the pure joy of being 'in company'.

The words flowed from me as if I were a vessel; it is an amazing experience, they fill the mind and the senses before they hit the page, and at times with such a sense of 'pure' love, that you just want to stay in the space, just a moment or two longer.

It is a most incredible and powerful experience - both for this vessel and I hope for you, the reader - and can result in a euphoric sense of being; combine this with pure humility and a sense of wholeness is created.

Thus, these inspirational messages, this guidance may result in a shift of energy; which may trigger a deep emotional response; it may clarify personal issues and create a sense of healing.

> *"Share the words with those who*
> *would listen. For in this too we learn."*

(NF 28/3/1998)

In love and light – you and I, journey together.

N.J. Fenttiman

The Committee

When I had been writing for some time, and had begun to move past the self-doubt, I was able to accept that the message, the wisdom, was beyond my conscious thought. The words just seemed to flow free of my consciousness.

It was at this point, I posed the question – "Who are you?" In reply the impression I received was of a group of beings, each with a specialty area of wisdom. The group would commune in unison – as one voice. However, if a specific explanation, or further detail was required, then 'the specialist' would step forward.

"It is with joy we greet thee,
and would commune with thee in unison.
We are many and would pass to thee words of love and of joy."

(NF 8/2/2001)

Thus in the reading you may be, at times, aware of the various tones and voices that come forward. The hint of an Irish lilt; the rhythm of a drum or heart beat; the gentle tone of a wise teacher or indeed the feeling and sense, within your heart of the pure unconditional love of a higher being – perhaps your own Guardian Angel.

And so, I opened to all of the impressions of 'The Committee'.

> *"Is it not more joyful to stand in company?*
> *As we who stand with thee."*

(NF 3/11/1997)

In love and light, always.

Inspiration

Yes child, we again welcome your company and bid you good morning. Each day brings new life and new inspiration to those who may be aware and open to that which is about. There is much to be aware of, and to take into ones psyche. To expand the whole being we must remain ever alert. Open to all knowledge, that each may take from the knowledge that which is necessary and appropriate at the time, or indeed at the specific moment. We cannot possibly absorb all knowledge, but if we remain closed and indifferent, we miss that which we require for our life's purpose, and in that missed opportunity we neglect our own potential and the development we strive for.

We may choose to let life flow over and by us, but not to grab hold, may at a later time fill our mind and heart with regret. Grab hold, the ride may be bumpy but it is living and in the living who knows what wonders are ahead. For indeed there are many to be experienced and to be absorbed, into our very being. Remembering to maintain balance, this with that, that with this and so on, and so on. Always balance life.

Do we not call to us, that which we need? And yet, too often we then neglect or ignore that which has come to our bidding. It is difficult at times to recognise the information or activity, as it may be in a symbolic form. Therefore, be aware of the moments of the day, for there is much wisdom held within the moment. Do not go in search, just be aware and be open to that which rushes by. Then, be prepared to take hold or capture, that which is yours for the tending.

Hold fast to the small blessings for they grow into larger wisdoms and joys. Behold that which is yours, for the glory of all is there for the sharing and you are a worthy being. One with all, in The One. We do not often recognize the connection, we do not often feel a worthiness to be of the connection, but know that in all we are connected. Each is a special piece of the whole. No one, no piece is too small, nor insignificant.

We are as one, we are one.

The Moment

All who are gathered here, send light and love to thee, and would take pleasure in your attendance. Those who gather - gather in light, love and wisdom and there is much to share with thee and those about thee. Wouldst thou attend?

Yes

Then so be it. We say to thee this morning all is well and is as it may be. Each movement at present is as deemed and is, as in the time - correct. Change comes to many. Noticed and unnoticed it occurs, for it is as needs be. That which we are afraid of is often only in the mind, do not go with fear upon its path. Fear leads one astray. Stay focused in the way and let fear pass thee by unattended and alone. You and yours walk in light, and need take no note of fear.

For a time there may seem 'about', that there is chaos, but it is indeed a show of energy and shall settle into peace and calm. The earth stretches and those upon it itch with anticipation. Scratch the itch and be content. There is joy and love in abundance for all if they but look about. Not in things but in the self and in others who share, one with another. We forget the basics. We forget the beauty of simplicity. We forget the being in silence.

Reach out into each moment, as in the touching we join with the moment and are part with it, not separate from it.

In time and in being we are one, as are all. Reach out and touch those who join in the same moment, a moment of existence, a moment of pure being. Be then always as one and live in this state of being and knowing, as in all, as of The One.

At this time child, just be. That which you need comes to the door. Know that which is, is, and the way ahead clears.

Now, let us enjoy the day and each moment of the day. Knowing all is as it may be, and that those who attend thee are at hand. We attend in love and light, and in joyful harmony, those who are aware and those in ignorance and despair. If they but know, there is no need of despair. In time, those who know shall begin, as it has begun, to reach out in wisdom and in joy. Thus, light and love shall pervade all. Darkness shall have nowhere to hide.

Together

It is good that we may sit once again. We come in joy and harmony to greet you and those about you. For is it not, a joyous occasion to gather together to share experiences and knowledge? We rejoice in this meeting of minds and souls, and as such shall share with each the wisdom of the days.

The smallest article, object, feeling and/or the smallest deed, goes not, unattended. Be it known, that the smallest of the small is known and is loved. Nothing and no-one is lost, neither it, nor they are forsaken. It is only fear and self-doubt that makes it seem so.

We in the universe are not hampered by darkness, all may be seen, as all may be heard. We note the rumblings of the furthest mountain and the babbling of the smallest brook. Know then, each one of you is known and heard. You, have but to ask and then to trust in the asking. Each of you may be what you will, it is but for you to trust and know that you have the power of love within to create your own will. We may guide, if asked and we may temper the way if asked, but we cannot do the deed. For it is your choice. However, we are with each in all things and we may hold back the barriers once the choice is made.

For the barriers are of the mind and of the heart, often placed so for protection. Then forgotten as to the why, and set in place now seem difficult to shift. They are but our own illusions and may be wiped clean from the place. As simply as opening the mind and heart to light and to love.

Ritual

You are here, as are we, at this moment in time and it is good to once again, join in the ritual of greeting. Ritual allows one to be in that moment and to focus the whole being. Too often, our focus strays and we become scattered. Thinking and doing too many things at one time, or rather trying to.

Ritual not only helps us to focus, it centres the being in the moment. The being, becomes the central point of the focus, thus allowing all that is to come to the being. Allowing one to take from the all their needs for the day. At this focal point, each dwells in the now and all energy and wisdom is focussed on the centre, and the you that is within this point, has the power of the ages to hand.

Scattered we begin to flounder, to wobble on our axis and cannot in this state grasp the opportunities that surround our being. Centre the self, focus the energy of thy being and be a part of the wisdom and love that you rightfully are. To do this may require rituals, routine, practice and participation in each and every moment. Remembering also, that in rest we participate in all else. Rest, relaxation and meditation are moments in which, that which escapes our grasp, may be caught and held and thus acted upon, if needs be.

Remember, that which is needed comes to the door, and

we need only be *at home* to receive it. Be open. Be aware. Do that which may ensure true balance at all times. In the balanced state, we exude calm and it is thus carried to others, who in turn may be re-balanced and thus exude calm, and so on and so on. Having spread thus, it becomes a powerful tool of light and love, for all to access and be part thereof.

Go, about the day, in peace and in the now.

Sharing

Good morning and greetings - Let us begin. Love does conquer all, though many have forsaken love. There comes a time when they shall turn to love and the ways of love. In addition, there shall be those who shall guide them.

It is time to re-awaken the sleeper, those who came with the knowledge but have been at there rest. They shall be up to the tasks ahead, for they know deep within that which is true, and they shall be led, and they shall be guided. No one walks this path alone. Memories shall awaken, knowledge shall awaken and they shall act upon the truth. They have chosen and they have been prepared.

Fear not, this all seems so serious and it is, but it is the seriousness of finding truth and love, and of accepting it thus without fear or question. To receive the gift openly and joyfully without suspicion. Suspicion has often dominated the receiving of a gift. Why do they give it? What do they want in return? It is time now to accept the gift, for itself and in the sense of giving, in the trusting of the giver.

Do you, each of you, trust the gift you have been given? The gift of love deep within. In addition, do you not trust in the sharing of this gift with others? For you are now called upon to go forth and share your gift of love, with all who come into your contact - obvious and not obvious.

When we feel emotions and acknowledge a knowing

thought, is there not a rush of energy and desire? Desire to get on with living and to move forward with the flow of the emotion. However, our fear kicks in and the moment is lost. Alternately, we could take hold of the moment and go with it. Trust and take a chance.

In all, have trust and faith, then in turn be about the business of the day. Holding to the self, each precious moment in recognition of the Great One in all things.

Sit Awhile

All clouds pass. Child, it is just a matter of time and trust. Sometimes we are unable to see ahead, but again we trust. It is best at these moments to sit quietly and take our rest. For all is in hand and as it should be. Sit awhile by the wayside and take note of who passes thee. Remember, there is learning and indeed answers in many guises.

Sometimes, there is a need to go in search and at other times; there is a need to sit, and to allow the searcher and the search to come to thee. Those who seek, shall find. Those who ask have help, and those who give of the heart, shall receive. Do not turn away from the gift. For you are worthy, as are so many.

Come together, in the love and light of The One in all and together, all fear shall be conquered and we shall again move as the whole, as one in true harmony. Harmony of the breath in all life, shall be found and exulted. One with the other shall recognise the worth of each, in all life. This worth shall be weighed in respect of all. No one shall fall away from sight, as all of life is precious, one to another in all things and in all ways.

Rejoice in the harmony of life about thee, and take energy and courage, from the life that abounds and surrounds thee.

Rejoice

Good morning.

We are here child, but a thought away. Feel the energy that is around you, and allow it to uplift your spirits, that you may know and cherish the essence of the day. Let the heart fly free. Let it soar on high with the angels, allow them to lift you higher than before and trust in their presence. Trust in that which they may show you, as we can learn so much from others.

Throughout your day, be still occasionally, that you may touch the grace and love that is about you. Feel this energy, and acknowledge the notion of time standing still, just for a mere instance. We each have the power to feel this connection, for we are as one, all connected. Neither a tear nor a smile goes unattended. Rejoice child in the energy of life about you, as we rejoice in your energy - the vibrations of life that you emit, and are in a greater way, part of.

With regard to the sensations of this energy, it need not be a thundering revelation; it may be the soft touch of a feather upon the cheek. Whichever sensation you experience, it is and always will be, an all-encompassing field of energy that you and all others generate and maintain. There are times when the energy may feel low or indeed depleted, *it is not,* this is but humanness interfering with the sensory terminals. At these times, trust and know you are en-cloaked always in the energy of love, and in the energy of eternal grace.

Thank you.

Rare Gifts

We greet you, child of light, and would share a word or two with you. We sit in friendly gesture with you and many others at this time for there is much to do and much to learn. As learners, we sit together in silent reverence and listen. As teachers, we share the knowledge we hold, from the heart.

Listening and sharing, are rare gifts to behold and as such, need nurturing in those who are prepared to go forth upon the plane. To take up the pole and traverse the way. Thus, upon this way, to take in the knowing that is shared and to scatter forth the seeds of wisdom, as ye pass along the way. Holding, not tightly to the self but being prepared to pass on the gifts, that which have been shared. In the grace, that they were shared with thee.

For example, a sunbeam cannot be held to the heart, although it may touch this precious space. Just as it touches thee, so it may be called to the attention of one who may not yet have noticed its strength and beauty and in so, touch another. The calling to notice is the passing of the gift. Having received the beauty, we desire to share this with another.

Is it not wondrous, that gifts may abound in places of obvious intent? And yet, they are often overlooked by this obvious placement. We were not always meant to be searching. We forget to just accept that which is at hand. For each in itself is a gift, as are each one of you. You child are a gift to thy world. Without each one of you, or indeed without just one of you, there would be such a void in the existence of all that is. Each is a gift to another. A lesson and a teaching to another, and so it is and so it shall be

For example, the coldness of the toes - the extremities, calls attention to the *whole*, and their need for care, and so one calls to another throughout the universe for care. Therefore, being put on notice we take action. We warm the toes, as we would care for the caller in time. Perhaps we are the caller, the distant extremity that needs love and care, and thus the whole reaches out with care and loving protection.

We need to once again appreciate, that each breath is a gift, and that as such, must be cherished, used and shared wisely. Not only with and for the self but with all of those about us. They in turn may receive or reject. Know you have done as needs be done, if you have opened the heart and the way of things, to the self and others. It all seems difficult and confusing, but it is as the ray of the sun that you, each one of you and of us, need only shine forth as the smallest ray of light, that it may light a dark passage, for the traveller and indeed for the self. Each may share in the lighting of their own passage to wisdom and grace. For is the gift not greater, for the personal participation in its creation and acknowledgement? Remembering, we are all connected and therefore in all we are one. Do we not see, that we create the gift we receive, we share and indeed perhaps that we reject? And so it is as it should be. Each one is part thereof.

A Destination

That which is within, is such a great part of the existence we know, and yet often we do not recognise this factor.

As the leaves flutter, so too, thoughts fly about and abound upon the plane. Beware the unguarded thought, for each is powerful. Thought may represent good or evil, light or dark, positive or negative and so on. Be aware of your thoughts and to whom they are aimed, even to the self. Always be positive in your attitude and thinking. Do not let dark and negative thoughts falsely empower you, for they have no feet. And thus sinking, try to take your energy and trust with them into the darkness, the plane of fear. The positive thought no matter how small buoys you and holds you safe upon the way.

Do not question the length of the journey, instead enjoy it and the many wonders upon the way. You may have a destination in mind, but often once begun, the journey may advance in a different direction. Be open to new and diverse destinations, and note that a destination is but a starting point, for the journey's next phase.

Does not the prospect of a journey, mental or physical, excite the whole of ones being? The energy rises, enthusiasm expands and feet itch, so to speak. Be prepared, for it may start at any time. Are you prepared? If we call, will you come upon the journey? There is much to do and we need the company.

A Light Ahead

Good morning, child, it is good to speak with thee. In thought and deed we are as one, we must be about the needs of others, as many struggle to find their way. Those that have found their path must light the way for those who seek. We each have duties and responsibilities, and in the processing of such we grow in strength and love and thus look back to share with those who follow. And yet, they do not follow, they but seek as we have done.

It gives one strength to see a light ahead and to know it represents a destination, or stopping point along the way. And light, may be another's achievement or indeed another being, one that we respect and acknowledge, as being of grace and love. This then gives the seeker cause to proceed in their quest, as the other appears as a welcome beacon.

Light & Dark

Send light that those who turn may see and seek. Let us speak today of light, for it seems that within light lies peace, hope, joy and all that we desire. But, light is just the half of dark, and in all life we need and must maintain balance. There is no harm in darkness. The dark night, when the moon is hidden offers no harm, it is only when the *power of fear pervades* our senses and we allow fear space, that darkness falls from balance.

Light your way child, as we light the way ahead and thus in light, trust the dark and know thy light is within and that it always shines for thee, as for each being. That which is within cannot be stolen, but in fear, we can give it up. Stay balanced, stay centred, and be who you are. Just be, in the now. Learn to again trust the self. Trust your instincts, the inner knowing that we occasionally set aside. Walk as one, as a whole being in tune with the self and with nature. Be in tune with life, as a *whole*.

Many souls gather at this time, for there is a need to band together in faith and trust, that all may be well, as we move forward with and into the new energy field. A field of clear thinking and consciousness. Cling to faith, faith in the self as a being of wholeness with and in the One in all, and trust your inner knowing. Act upon your instincts and urges and go forward in this knowing of being one with all.

No one is separate, no one is alone, no one is isolated. We are all one, we are of the One. It is so.

These writings may seem serious in tone, but it is just that things move on and learning, jumps forward a notch or two, or three. In learning, there is wisdom and in words, there is meaning. All shall be clear, and then the perceived serious aspect, shall fall away.

Although we speak as one, often the tone of the speaker, on the day, may present an aspect, you are not yet comfortable with, but in time, this comfort and security of knowing shall also balance out. We learn, child, as you learn, and new experiences and perceived situations have to be negotiated. We *all*, in the moment experience this negotiation. It is fun to stretch one's self into a new suit, do you not feel it so? Thus, experimenting with various energy fields, and you are such on energy field. You had not perceived yourself as such, but all life animate and in-animate is energy. And there are many varieties of energy, as yet, not perceived. But you awaken. For what is in the heart, is pure and of pure intent and thus a clear channel of progress may be created and utilised. For if, the heart is pure so too is the mind and the soul of the being.

Thus, draw from that which is in your heart, and trust.

Reach Out

Dear Friends, beauty is unto the beholder, everlasting, and the work at hand brings beauty into the lives of many, who feel forsaken upon the way. And in the knowing, they shall rejoice in their new found trust and love of all, and of the self.

For they, shall rejoice and pronounce their inner knowing to all who may listen. In addition, in their pronunciation, many shall be drawn to the inner joy of trust and love, with and in all living beings, and so, shall they all share one with another, and so on and so on, as it shall be.

We speak of joy, love and beauty, and of a time, when all may share in the living of all things. Reaching out, one to another without fear or suspicion. A time, when once again hearts and minds may open to the 'what is' in all, and so, to be part again of the whole. No longer as isolated beings, we may connect one with another for the greater good of all living beings. Thus, letting the energies mix and overflow, in faith and trust. Relying fully on the intuitive knowing, now again opening to The All, and to each in The All.

So be it.

A Shift

Yes child, do you hesitate in fear or in anticipation? Perhaps the later for there is nothing to fear and the period of hesitation draws to an end. Yes, much about you, is at this time fluid and you seem to be travelling with the flow but as yet, not moving.

This is so, for each journey needs preparation and it is we, with your higher agreement that have been preparing the way. And that is why, you have felt and acknowledged the change in energy and the sense of shifting that has been in evidence on the physical plane about you.

Soon, all shall be made clear, and the sense of hesitation and anticipation maybe converted to forward propulsion and directed energy. The excitement builds. Each, thus ready to move out upon their knowing way, shall take up the challenge and go ahead. That they may smooth the way for others, perhaps a little slower upon the way, yet, protected and guided by the light.

Each journey has a starting point, and upon the way, there are many destinations. We may rest at these, or we may choose to stay, or perhaps to stay only awhile. Then, the destination becomes a platform, from where to commence the next stage of the journey - remembering, we have - choice.

Each journey is different, and each *being* is different,

however, each is noted upon their way and accompanied. Each connected with the One and of the One in all. So many differences and yet, within we are all of the Source.

Often, what appears to be turmoil, is but the stretching out of the feathers and the shaking of the dust from the back. 'Great Eagle' stretches out wings of protection, over thee and as many others who would see the light, and love all, in all. And the reach is great, none shall be denied. They need but ask, and they shall be gathered forth within the fold.

Go now, upon your day.

Ancient Ones

We would speak, if you wouldst allow? Peace and tranquillity shall be a gift, that will flow around and before each of you; joy and love shall also spread forth. Just as the petals of a rose fall and blow about in the wind, so shall joy and love spread out. They shall glide upon the wind and they shall be welcome where they rain, for they are badly needed and in much need, as there are many at this time, which have turned their back on such, and will welcome you, and love, back into their lives again. It need only be introduced.

Each who now steps forward shall introduce these gifts, not only to themselves but also to others, for in the giving and in the sharing, so we receive. Just as we give and share, so shall you, and so shall they, and so it will spread outwards ever further. Ripple upon ripple, until it goes right around and comes back, and again around and back. In time growing ever stronger, each time growing ever more powerful.

There is much rejoicing, there is much laughter, and there is much joy.

** *** **

There is beauty about each and every one, if I may say so? And if I may, for a while continue as the voice of many? - You sit within the confines of the encampment of many. Many gather about, not only of the Indian Nations, but many other Ancient One's gather likewise, and sit thus in circles.

There is a beauty in the gathering, a softness, a peace and joy that goes and flows one to another and moves around as the rivers flow, and as the brook, gently flowing and passing one to another, not interrupted. This energy, this beauty often forsaken, stands ready to be absorbed, to be shared and those that gather, gather in the beauty and in the love, and in the desire of being as of and in the One, that each and all are connected.

The many, are all ages and of all beings, not just the 'human beings'. Many animals gather about, and they stand one with another, as with each. Those that do not stand, fly and circle about. And in the flow, so too the fishes; each and every type of living creature is represented in this circle. The colours of the universe, fill the sky and fill each and every one who is gathered and who gathers. Know that, each of you is part of this beauty, each of you is part of the circle, each of you is part thereof, one with, and all in the One.

We who gather thank you for allowing us to share this time and these words. And know always, that at any time we may be called forth, for we are always but a thought away.

Thank you.

Ask

Let peace and tranquillity surround and embrace you, for you are special. Know this, in your heart, you are of the light, you are a light being, here to bring joy to the many.

All is well, be at peace within the self and calm the waters about you. Be still and be quiet, for that which you need comes to you. Know, we are with you throughout time, and that which you wish is yours to have. We, work with thee in all things.

Fear not, child, and just be you. Go forth from here and enjoy the days ahead, you have much to learn and much to share. Know that others also learn from you. Do not feel inferior, each one is about their own journey and no one is better or greater, than the other is. You, are in good company as you journey, and if in doubt go within and look to your company.

Go now, with courage and strength.

Three Or More

Good Morning, child, we greet the day, we greet you. Is there not beauty all around?

Yes there is.

So too we speak of beauty. The beauty that is within and without, and around all things.

There is beauty in all, we have but to recognise it, and to acknowledge it. Beauty, is to all different, as we each perceive of it in different ways. What each individual acknowledges as beauty, may in fact not be acknowledged as beauty by another, but it is no less beauteous to the individual.

It is just, that we accept and acknowledge degrees of difference, in the seeing and in one another. Just know, that there is beauty everywhere, we have but to look, not only with our own eyes, but indeed also, in the use of our own senses.

Take for example, a stone, to one it may be a rare thing of beauty to the touch, as to the eye, yet, to another it is just a stone. To each his own way, his own vision, his own quest for beauty. Remembering, that in the quest for beauty, we learn so much about joy, and in joy we are led to love and contentment.

This may seem incredulous, yet, a small step, a small awakening, a small acknowledgement, may and does lead such a long way upon the path, to glory in the One. For it is here, that the core of true beauty lies, and it lies within all. It is not distant, it is not remote. We are all beautiful beings in the One, we are all of the One. We are the sum total of All That Is.

We, speak as one, of the gathering of the many. The time is now and many gather about in many citadels. Each starts from the citadel within, and each takes this sacred space in their travels. So that where they sit, they sit within the *citadel of time*. They sit in peace. We gather now in peace, and go forth from each gathering in peace.

In the gathering, each may share, without fear or favour and each, may open to the sharing process, for it is time to open, to share and to trust, for the All is greater than the one, but the one is indeed part of the All. Open and be truly of the One in all.

This is no time to hold only to the self. Be open, be trusting and give of the self. Know, that in being open, we not only give of the self but that we receive also, to the self.

No one is greater or smaller than another, we are but different, yet, we are not as different as we may perceive. Some may walk tall, some may wear feather or scales, some may walk upon four legs, or stand tall in one place - each and all has its place, even as we have ours.

Go forth, for now is the time to go ahead and be. Be as the self, in open and loving ways go forth and be. As each goes forth, so the gathering takes place, for each new pace brings us into contact with another, or others, who also, at this time go forth and gather. Share and pass on. And in thus, share and pass on, both in steps and in wisdom.

The ripples spread forth. You, are but of the ripple, and it does go forward and outward, from the heart stone.

Know, that as you, and each one of you, go forward, so too the heart stone knows thy path and threads it with love, joy and beauty.

Go now, go in peace. Amen.

Treasures

We greet the child, and the woman of light, for to us, we ever see the beauty and innocence of the child that is the woman.

Today we speak, not only to the child of light but to the woman also. It is time to be about the work that the woman must do, yet, do not lose sight of the child, for in the child is openness and pure joy, and we have much need of these treasures.

In going forth upon our set ways, there is much to be aware of and in this awareness we learn, and take in our dues. Having then digested the knowledge, we open outward and give of the knowing to others. Those nearest and those farthest receive, and in turn send out their knowing.

It seems as if we go in circles and so we do, for what is shared here is also shared elsewhere, as in the same instant. And for the time, repetition is used to lodge that which is necessary. Do not all foundations stand strong, to hold all, that may be placed upon them. So too, we build a strong foundation. That which is, spreads out to many and they then shall gather to share and re-enforce their knowing.

In the thought, in the word and in the doing, each is part of the whole and is thus, important. Just the knowing, of such an energetic wave is sufficient to each one, who then may spread this energy. It is too great to hold only to the self, but know, in the sharing, the thought, word and deed spread out further, than one may at this time perceive. And it is good, it is so.

It Passes

We wait. In turmoil, you face but a black cloud, and it is passing, all shall be well again. At these times rest or go with the feeling. Do not push against it so. These moments have reason as do others. All, in its place. If we are euphoric at all times, how would we know? For there would be no benchmark to compare, and yet, if we search our heart and mind, there is joy in most places. It is just that on occasion we do not recognise it.

Trust that which is, for we learn from each situation and in the learning, we grow in wisdom and joy. Even that which may seem a trivial nuisance, holds a lesson, if we but look to it.

Hope

Why is it, child, that you are often so hard on yourself, and yet, not on others? Are you less, or do you feel less important?

No, I just don't want to let anyone down, and it seems so often, I do.

Child, we all do what we feel is best, and that which comes from the heart, is of our best. Know, that you are as you are, and what you do and say is of your best. Often, it heals far more than you know. Do not change for you are, you. Pure of heart and deed.

We need the ear, mind and heart of many such as you, so as to be about the work at hand. Know, that when we perceive a failure, it may not be as it seems and it is, in no way your fault. It maybe, that the person is yet in transition, and not yet ready, to receive or relate. Just leave the seed and pass on, for there is much barren ground to cover. Know that that which is sown shall in time flower and then go on to spread more seed upon the way. No seed is lost, it may be ignored or refused, but it is not lost to sight. And in time, it shall find its ways to fruition. Hope, is not lost.

Never lose sight of hope, for in hope there is life eternal. So it is, so it shall be. Hold hope to the heart, and trust thy knowing.

Yet, do not fear this period of growth, it is as a child

grows, natural. And the process is natural, and of nature. Lean into the movement and flow with it, not against it.

Wonderment abounds, as does joy and beauty. Feel the energy of life all about thee and know all is well.

33

Patterns

A beautiful day.

Yes child, it is a beautiful morning, but know there is beauty in darkness. Just as you see the stars at night, so too, we see the souls of light, and they ever glow in beauty. Thought too, may be seen as rays of energy darting about, here and there, and to and fro. Weaving patterns as they criss-cross one another.

The threads of gossamer fill the airways creating wondrous patterns of thought, which in turn become wondrous deeds and actions, and fact. A wondrous thought, a wondrous deed, needs to be shared. Open thy heart and thy hands, and hold forth that which is, to all who may share of it.

This period of time, is not for holding only to the self, it is the time for all to open forth to others. Some may wish to count the profits, but they are uncountable, for in the opening up of the self to all that is, the gifts are great indeed. They may not be calculated, it is not a time to calculate, and some shall fall away as they may need to see the profit. It is so, it shall be.

By opening to all that is, we open to that which we cannot see or feel, to that which is at present, hidden from our sight. But know, it is hid no longer, for as ye open, so ye shall again see, hear and feel all that is. And that which is, is close about thee, even as now.

So much again flows forth, that it is, as of a river rushing to the sea, but in the rush, the river touches many. For instance as it swirls around a bend, or flattens out upon the planes, so the many are greeted and rewarded by the flow, and in turn, they pass on the rewards to others. Then on into the sea, to reunite again with the All, and then again to regenerate the rivers flow, and so the cycle goes and shall ever go, for as long as needs be.

Thank you.

Preparation

Dear friends, what words of wisdom would you share with me today?

There is change about at this time for many. They know of it, yet, do not need to act upon it, for the present. Still, the preparations take place. But those affected, know there is change in the offing and they make note of the need. They however, do not yet see the direction to take, but all shall be made clear in time. The first step, and an important preparation, is the knowing of a need for change, this knowing or feeling allows us to begin to let go, to make ready for the next move or preparation, like juggling we must prepare and practice for the next move or action.

Often, it seems as if things go about the bush in circles, but in all things, there is a method and in this method, patience and understanding are not of the least, in the position of importance. All preparations must be carried out in great understanding of their place in the plan of things and all work must be directed with true patience. And thus, all goes ahead in love, and of love.

Do not doubt the self, for it is great indeed and has resilience yet untapped. Go forth as the person you are, and do great deeds, for it is in thy power to be as of the self and to go ahead in dignity and grace. You may stumble, occasionally upon the way, but there are no deep holes, and each recovery shall bring wisdom and joy. Do not go hardly, upon the self, know you are worthy and indeed prepared for the way ahead.

Open the door of your choice and step through to the beauty of love. A love grown strong over past times, a love that enfolds and encompasses all that you are, to the self and to all about thee.

Thank you.

Take Note

It is good, that messages be sought upon the way, and that they in turn may be shared with others. Take note, that those others may also, have messages to share with thee. Greet each day and each one with open arms, and open heart that what each, may have to share and impart may be welcome without constraint.

That which you need, is within. You need only to look within and draw out what is appropriate, for that moment and so it shall be.

Always look, to the I Am that is within and without all that is in existence, for nothing exists without, I Am. The All that is, is of each, as each is of the All. And so it is, and ever shall be.

Oh, Great One we open our eyes to thee
We bow before thee
That which you are, so too we are
For without thee,
We are as of nothing.
Let us rest in thee, Great One
Let us bide with thee, in all things
We are of thee and in thee
In all that is, we are part with thee
So too Great One, we are.
Go now, in peace and be about your way.

Giving

All was still for a time, but now moves ahead. That which you fear shall not eventuate as the mind, the will and the knowledge comes together, as you open with ease and share thy learning. Trust and be thyself - open and caring.

Fear is not a factor in this equation, nor should it be.

There is such beauty in the wiles about you, such that you will have no difficulty seeing and knowing, and it shall touch not only the conscious self, but also the silent inner self.

All that you are, has led to this moment in time, and you are well prepared for the journey and the tasks ahead. The chains, that have held thee now fall away, although in some instances reluctantly, yet, they fall. But the memories live on and remain in friendship and joy.

Walk with 'bear' at thy side, find the silence and still the being. It is from the stillness, that life may flow forth, un-impeded by our distractions. Be still, be calm and trust in what you are, for you are, of the One. That which you seek, shall be shown to you, and know you walk in light, and that you are about the business, of the One.

You asked to work for and with spirit, and you do. You shall continue upon this way, even if at times it may seem hard. However, you shall have periods of rest, to reflect and restore, and to then again have choice. For life, is made up of choice and of experience, but we may choose the experience and the degree to which we may participate, in the experience.

Do not cheat the self, by giving of less than your best, for it is in this giving, that we gain in learning and wisdom.

All That Is

We speak to you today, of all that is.

That which is, is of the self and of all that surrounds thee. Look also to the land, to nature and to all things of earth and sky, and of sea and air. All that is , is of the All, as so too, are we.

Come within and be guided by the knowing. That which dwells within, rises up to greet the new day. Be prepared for this moment of knowing, and greet it with full and hearty welcome. Do not draw back, do not waver upon the decision, but instead boldly step forward to greet that which is, that which awaits you.

Step out from where you are, into a shower of such sunlight, as to embrace the universe in full vision, upon the way of wisdom and light. And such shall be your journey, showered by rays of sunlight, sparkling as jewels upon thy path and even as to the night, lighting your way as day. And so it shall be as you traverse the way ahead, moving ever forward upon a straight way. Know, the brambles are cleared from thy way. Go with the wisdom that is, for the wisdom of old rests gently upon they shoulders.

That, which is unseen and unknown troubles thee not, for all that ye shall need shall be seen and known, nothing shall be hidden nor indeed difficult to seek out. You have the gift, the way of things, upon your hands and heart. You need but to trust, and reach out your gifts to others. And it shall be so. In all that you do, so too, you shall reach forth for others, and thus for the wisdom of self.

Go, in light and reach forth.

Challenge

In your gatherings (meditation groups), each has a part to play, and each part in turn has merit. Thus, each now steps forward to take up the challenge of the wisdom. The wisdom of old is re-awakened and now must be acknowledged. Those who accept the challenge and make their way forward, will do so in love, light and trust, and in this way, they then shall light and lighten the way ahead, for others to follow.

It is time for each to know their way, and to walk it, in full view of the All. The Great One knows and sees all, and now we acknowledge this wisdom.

We, also step forward, as this journey begins and each in turn walks with thee. We walk as many, but now it is time to begin the journey of knowing, and we each have teachings and knowledge to share. As it is needed, or required we may step forward, each in turn to share with thee that which is required, your task then shall be to share this learning with those about thee.

Angels walk lightly by thy side, and teach you of the gentle ways, so that in all things you tread gently. And yet, strength and courage are ever your allies. Hold the head proud, child, at all times, yet remember those at thy feet. Walk tall, stepping not on others, walk as they may have time to step aside. There is no need for rush in the period ahead, for each part of the way is set and shall in turn be identified and recognised for its part, in all that is.

Go in peace and love, and be the self in all things. All that is, is in thee and about thee. All that is, is in all things. Look to the beauty and wisdom in all. Look to the way of the All.

Go lightly, go well.

Love & Joy

Child, we are ever with thee and would speak of love and joy. The love and joy one feels and shares with others, for is this not how it should be? When we experience a moment of pure joy, we wish to rush out and share this with another, as this is the way of things. Even in nature, joyous moments are shared. All that is, knows this need and makes provision for such, in each of our lives.

It is we, who often ignore or neglect the feelings of joy. And so we become morose and sad, yet, there is no need for such feelings of despair, as each thought even as to the negative may be turned to joy. For joy is in its shadow and would stand forward into the light, if thus invited.

Remember, that which is, may be changed if we but put in a little effort. We have the power to make change, it is our gift from the Great One. We need, but recognise the gift, and then to utilise it for the *good of all*. Then indeed joy shall be ours to have, to hold and to share.

We have no need to give it away, we need only to share the joy and the gift of giving with others. Remembering always to hold some to the self, for it is an offence to the Giver of life, to neglect our share of the joy.

In the knowing and sharing of joy there is true love, and it is within all to know love, and the beauty of love. It is our gift, our right to know and to experience love, and to thus in turn, share this knowing, and this experience with others and with those about us. Forget not those near to us. When reaching out, do not overlook those nearest as often happens, for we take these for granted, as they us.

Perhaps, we need to re-connect with those nearest, on a more regular basis, so as to recognise their joys and indeed their pain. For at times, one goes not without the other ,and those nearest need to be aware, so as to offer a hand in peace, if it is required.

Just, as we in spirit reach out a hand in peace, so too, man must again reach out to one another in peace, love and joy without the thought of profit or gain. Else, all may be lost to sight, in their way ahead.

Need For Change

Good morning, dear friends.

Yes, child, it is a good morning and we gather, here in spirit and upon the earth plane, just as many gather throughout the universe at this time.

The time ahead, may seem confusing at times for some and yet, things are as they may be. We have had time, to place that which is needed in order and now it must be put in motion. Those who gather hence shall have the tools at hand to work for the love of all, for it is in this use of love, that what is to be, may indeed be brought to fruition.

Many now awaken, to that which they know to be of necessity and they shall hasten to their tasks. For all about, there is change and need of change. Those who fight against the change shall have times of difficulty and loss, yet, those who move lovingly with it, shall have all that is at hand, for their means and for that of those about them.

Do not fear child, as you look about the earth, for it is the changes within that we speak of. Too often, we neglect the inner knowing and it is now time to acknowledge and accept this wisdom. It is time, to trust this knowing and to act upon its directions and guidance. This is not a tool that leads one astray, it is indeed the word of the One in all and we have but to be still and listen, as the word is not a whisper. Yet, it is in the stillness that we shall hear and know the word of God – the creator of all that is.

Many tremble at the word 'God', yet, it is deeply embedded in all cultures and in all beings, they have but different ways of speaking and thinking these *sounds*. But for all, it is time to go within and listen, by whatever mode as may be necessary, and at this time throughout the universe, so it shall be.

Go now about thy day, remembering always, to listen to that which is within, that which now seeks recognition and action. Share what is, with those about thee, and be surprised by that which is returned. For others, now begin to recognise the essence of the many, just as you also recognise their essence.

Go in peace, light and love.

Thank you.

Foundation

We are with you, little one, although at times, we may seem a little quiet and distant, yet, we are ever with thee. That which you know in your heart, and in your inner being grows stronger and more powerful each day. Time gathers all, even to the creatures of the earth, for all beings are now called to the way of the One, that each may share their wisdom and knowing with the other.

For child, in the unity of all there shall be peace. One with another may join in harmony and love, that they each may know the other in truth and in love, and thus in peace. True peace rests within the harmony of all, but each must now seek the way of peace. Too long, man has strived for self to the deterrent of all else, but now man sees the errors, and in truth may now turn things about.

Remember always, we each have choice. No one is asked more of, than can be clearly and willingly accomplished. Each achievement, no matter how small it may seem, is of importance for the self and for the whole, for each small act becomes the foundation of change, and in change 'what is' may take its place, in the scheme of all that is.

Go, knowing your place in the all is guarded and held safe.

Let Go

It is a peaceful time child, is it not? Know that all is well with thee and indeed with those about thee. You have come far child, and yet still, there is a way to go. For the present, all seems quiet, but you have much to do and learn, and we wait and watch quietly, thy progress.

Know that, all things work mysteriously and yet, together. Although at times it seems as if we pull in different directions, it is the self that pulls against the flow. Sometimes it is best just to let go, and go, that we may learn by that which comes by, or by that which we brush by. Always be aware of that which brushes by, touching one's life ever so gently, and yet, unnoticed we may miss an opportunity of great importance. That, which touches us in gentle strain, is often, that which we may need or desire, do not always expect to be hit, by a lightning bolt. Yes, lightening certainly gets the attention desired. But is it our desire, or that of another? Remember, the gentle touch, and be aware, it takes more effort, but the results are rewarding, to say the least.

There are, so many things to say and share, and yet, often time allows for only a word here or there. Yet, know that each word or shared experience may be filled, with many messages, it is but, for one to analyse the word or experience. Roll the knowing about in the mind and the heart, and savour the sound, the sense it ignited, the smells and extra sounds it provoked, and the intuitive knowing that hence, was awakened. What may at first, seem simple and insignificant, may in fact be large and of import, intent. This is how, a greater sense and knowing of wisdom, may be shared in a single word, or in a brief moment,

Note, the reaction you have to a word, a sound, a smell, a scene, a person and so on. There may be much hidden from the eyes view, yet, there to be discovered by a discerning being. This is a gift we all have, yet so often neglected and ignored. It is time for such as the self, to at last acknowledge and practice this gift, this talent, this knowing, and it is indeed an inner knowing of old, and we are all attached to this knowing. We may all have access to it, it is, but a remembering of how to access this hidden talent. Know, it rises to the surface, and may be encapsulated for the use of all and self, alike.

Yet, in the use of such talent and knowledge, remember always, to respect the others point of view, for their position on certain matters may be varied. Step gently upon the way, but always proudly, with head held high.

Go, in peace and light, all thy days. Amen

Community

Good evening.

Child, it is time to work and work you shall, but it shall be of an enjoyable and specific nature. That which is about you, is strong and of an important nature. That, which you may learn in this place, shall carry with you, in all your future ways. Know there are many ways upon your chosen path, yet, you know this way and the need for wisdom upon this path. Each of the ways, shall reveal its time and presence when needed, and those who may have influence or knowledge, shall be revealed at such times. They in their turn shall aid thy way and guide thy path.

Look not, to those just of the earth for guidance, but those also of the skies, both night and day. And as those who seek thy help, find their way to your door, so you shall have the guidance and wisdom that may, at the time be needed. There are many who walk with thee, and they together and as individuals, shall be with thee in silence or when called. Know we are ever with thee, yet, in times of special need we shall heed they call.

What is, is and always shall be, yet we as thinking beings hold the power of change within our hearts and minds. Yet, many use this power in false, and selfish ways, to create true change for the good of all, we must think and do the deed, with open and pure hearts and minds. There must be, thought for others and also for the consequences of our thoughts and deeds. Remember, ultimately, we pay the consequences, of our thoughts and actions.

Purity and innocence, may influence the way of what is. We must return, to a childlike innocence, remembering the gifts we brought with us to this world of ours, for we each came, equipped to make a difference and to right the wrongs. Not in a grand way, but in our own unique individual way, and yes, we can each make a difference, be it small or large is of no great consequence to the self, for it is the deed, regardless of size that is of true importance, and of course, the way in which the deed is carried out. Each shall judge his or her own attitude to the deed, and to their reasons, for participating in the thought or act, which ever maybe required at the specific moment in time.

And it is these moments, these windows of opportunity, which may or may not make the difference, when acted upon, to the great what is. Are you prepared to act, when called upon? And in what attitude, that of self or community (community - being of all life, of all that is) shall you act? We ask this not just of thee, but of all thinking beings, and shall they be counted? Shall they be prepared, to look back to innocence and remember, what it is, that they know and carry within? For it is a great task, and a great responsibility to walk upon this path to wisdom and light, and many find this responsibility too great a burden.

Go now, child, it is time to rest.

Thank you.

Just Think

That which is, child, shall and always will be, although at times we may lose sight of the Great One. And at times also feel that the Great One loses sight of us. Yet know, we are never lost, nor lost from sight. There is always one, and often many who watch over each being. Just, as the children are cared for and watched over, so too the Great One watches over all, even to the smallest of all living creatures.

We who fear the silences and the periods of aloneness should not, for in these times of peace we are nearest to All That Is and may, if we so desire, connect with ease at such times. We may, in such connecting be as one, with The All, and thus be able to open to and absorb all the wisdom that is available to the self, in such a moment of peace and oneness. And thus, we shall learn not to fear the self and the oneness of self, for at such times we are indeed whole in the self, and in, and with all that is about us.

Just think, all of this energy and power is available to each individual being, yet, many do not realise all that is to hand, if they but be still, and reach out from within, in peace, and in love of all. But no, too few trust the self and even fewer reach out in peace. They do, however, reach out in times of fear, and those who are about are glad to be of help, yet, think of the help that is truly available at all times, if they would but reach out. It is the fear of reaching inward first, that many cannot face, they are *needlessly* afraid to face the self, for it *is* only the self that must be faced.

The monsters they fear are of their own creation. They are not of the All, nor shall they ever be. These monsters do not exist, it is the strength that we give to fear, that creates these imaginary creations, these monsters of ours.

Be Still

Child, we are ever here and speak often, in your ear and in your heart. Yet, you know and understand this. Each one who would sit a moment and still their day, would realise how close they are to All That Is, and in the realisation, they would be in touch with All That Is. In the touching, they then may reunite the self with all else, and know they are a part of the whole. Each being, is an important part of the whole, yet, they forget this and search endlessly for that which indeed they know. Yet, they search outwardly, when in fact all they seek is within and they need only to look to the all-knowing self that is with, and within them, always. For each is part of the other, and of the whole and in this each is of the One. For what is, could not be, without, what is not. Thus, go within and realise the full potential of the self.

Then, in the realisation of self, each may share this knowledge and wisdom with others about them, that they too may find the stillness and the self. In the unity of self, we find peace. For whom then, with and in the state of oneness with self, could trouble another? Why, in the oneness of self we know and experience all, do we resist and fight against this union? Yet, if we find this union so difficult, why are we ever searching? Are we afraid of our own knowing and of the peace that recognition shall bring?

Have we become so comfortable with fear and doubt? Yet, we know, we require neither.

It seems here, that we go in circles, and we do, for we ever run and hide from that which we seek. It is we, ourselves, who make the journey to self so difficult, when in fact it is so simple. Sit still, and be all that you are. Be of the self in all things, and be the self to all that is about and within thee. There is no need of fear, nor of courage, just be. Be as the flowers and open the self to the All, then again we are as one, in and with the One from whom, all that is and all that is not, comes forth to each.

Self-Realisation

Child, it is, as if but a moment has passed, since we last spoke. Know, that all who are in need, received that which they ask for. Yet, often that which they seek is right before them, they need but look. Too often, life crowds in and we are unable to look about and see what is there, that which is truly of our calling.

All too soon, we forget from whence we come and to whence we are headed. The journey between, is that, a journey of self and of self-realization. The realisation that the self is a being of relevance and of beauty. A being of love and of joy. A being of power and energy. All the ingredients, of being self. We do not have to be recreated by others. We have only to be, and in being, trust the self and the knowledge and feelings of self.

Why do we not trust the self? Yet, we are prepared to trust others, and alter the self to please and vindicate the wishes of others, as they would mould and re-shape the ever-wonderful being before them. Why, do we give our power and beauty away? Why, do we allow others to mould us, to their way? Take the self to task, and stand up for the being, that you are.

By giving our power away, we harm not only the self, but those also to whom we relinquish it. This then, is a travesty of justice and in thus, shall cause pain to the self and to the other.

Know then the self and be the self as each is meant to be. In being truly the self we, harm no other, nor the self. Again, we come to trust. Can each being truly learn to trust the self? That which they are, and that which they may, and can be.

Be the self, in all things.

Touch The Stars

Fly high, child, and touch the stars, and know we are ever with thee. That which may seem difficult at times, passes without incident quite often. Know that what is, is and that most events have a way of balancing in the end. For one thing leads to another, and we must not falter, at the various steps of the procedure.

Do not take on, that which is not yours. Each one must carry their own responsibilities, desires and deeds. Each, must face their own way. We may guide and we may respond to requests for help, but in the event, each must make their own way in life. For it is that, that they experience. This is not to say, that along the way they may receive, and give, of loving and understanding ways and deeds.

Remember, *all* are the same, all are of the One and each must respect the other in all things. Know that in and with love, all things are possible. Send love to situations, which may seem difficult, and in this you also bring love to the moment in hand. This gift of love is a most powerful gift, and if *all* situations, both difficult and joyful, were steeped in love, then peace and joy would pervade the all, and in turn, they would go forth and share, of the love and joy, in all they do.

Do not, underestimate the power of love. For indeed this gift is meant for all, and the all may share in it, if they but open to love, and turn aside from fear.

Dear child, there is so much to say and share here with thee and others, yet, you block the way at times. Do not doubt the words you feel, set down all that you may, for it is in the personal translation that others shall find the love they need, or indeed strengthen the love they know.

Do not be put off, or aside, by the fears of others. For there is always hope, and the conscious energy of the hopeful is most powerful. We need but stay focused on positive energy, to bring about the positive changes to our world that we desire. Remember, that many gather and in the gathering, much may be accomplished for the good of all, in such gathering.

Yet know, this gathering may be physical, but need not be so. For it may be, that the thoughts and desires of many fly forth and gather as one most powerful, and in thus they may be gathered in, by the most powerful One.

For child, each has the power of the One within, and it is that, that with the connecting and the reconnect daily, we grow in knowing and in wisdom, and we learn in depth of the self and of the ways of the self, and of the power of the self. Many ask what can I do. Yet, as the true self we are most powerful, and we each know deep within, that we may make a difference, if we so choose.

You may seem confused child, but deep within the self, you have the knowledge to know and understand these words, and the energy and power of love, to act upon them, as do all beings.

Go forth now, in love and light, and spread joy to those you greet.

Sunbeam

The bells of light, gleam and glisten as the morning dew welcomes the day. So too, we bid thee welcome, for is not the new day glorious, in all its wealth of beauty and newness?

Each must find, within themselves the beauty and newness of self. That which awaits the discovery of being whole, is but a sunbeam away, for any who may look. And in the looking, truly see the self for what it is.

Sit still, as now, more often in the days ahead, that we may touch the being, and thus bring clarity of thought and nearness of heart. Then in so doing, the All shall open before thee and you may then dip into the knowledge and wisdom of old. Thus, you enhance the self and draw to the self that which is yours to have.

Then, in the knowing, you shall have clarity of thought and deed, and shall be able to guide those who ask the way. Do this gently, and answer only what is asked of thee, for each must tread their own path. Yet, help is ever at hand, and you may be asked for help, and in thus, give it.

Know child, the answers are within and as you help one, they in turn, help you and so it is meant to be. A word here, a deed there and always a smile as one passes by.

Just trust the self and be the self, for that is the greatest gift of all.

Re-Focus

Greetings. Everything that is about us, has the power and energy to share, and in the sharing, we are re-energized. We need but ask the help of nature and those about us. It need not, and should not be, that we give of the self and never take what is offered in return. Just reach out, and know you are worthy of all the love there is to receive. Then, in an overflow of love, you may reach out to others and share with them.

That, which is negative about thee, feeds on fear. Put fear aside, it has no place here. Do not nurture this energy, for it undermines, that which gives it space.

Take comfort in the knowing that what you do and what you are helps many, and that you in turn are loved. You child, are love, as are so many about you. Yet, often they too forget, they come from love and light, and that these dwell ever with, and within each. They need, but to re-focus and to re-explore, the sensation and the knowing.

Reach out the heart and hand, bring light and love to all you meet and know, you do not do this alone, as many walk with you in all spheres of your day. For that which criss-crosses thy path forms the very pattern of life and the experiences of life.

Go forth and make of the experiences all that ye may. Relax and draw peace to the mind, and to the heart . Fill these with light and love, and with the intent of glory to all.

Walk in gentle moccasins, and tread the path of beauty and joy. Know that all that is, is there to be utilised, and know all that is, is in and about you and each other, always.

Awaken

Greetings, we welcome your presence, amid this company of knowing and of wisdom old. They who gather welcome thee to their midst. Yet, you have never been absent, just veiled in the mists of time and forgetfulness, but now is the time to step into the clear way, and to remember thy wisdom.

There is no division in who has or hasn't wisdom, for it is with and in all beings. It is but the time of awakened use that differs in some. Yet now, it is time for many to reawaken, and those as yourself, awake that ye may guide others to their own strength and beauty of mind and soul.

This time has seemed off putting and testing, yet it is the self that sets these limits, for child, there are no limits. Teach this to those absent from thee, that they need not shackle their knowing and the gifts they each possess. For in shackling the self we restrict the flow of energy and wisdom, and now, is not a time for restriction and restraint, it is a time of growth and of forward motion.

Again, we say, step forward gently upon the way. Tread as not to break a single stick upon thy path, for you know not the reason it lays before or beside thee. Yet, you shall know, for as you traverse this path all shall be made clear to thee, and in such, also to those about thee. For there is much to learn, to experience and to recall. And the call now vibrates about the world, your world, and also about the universe of infinite time and love. Now, is the time to stand forth, and take thy place.

Know, you are ever guided by love and light, and in this, you shall guide. There is no fear upon this way, and that, that each shall have and share upon this way, shall be multitudes. All that is desired lays ahead for those who would reach out, in love, light and in peace. Being love and joy to the self, and those in whose company you keep. Visit not sadness and despair, nor visit it upon another.

In all things, know and seek light, walk in the light of love, knowing always the God of Light walks with thee, as the spark of life that you are. For *without*, we are as of nought.

Go now, about the business of your day, ever watchful of that which is with and about thee, and step gently into the day.

Always

Child of light and love, all goes well with thee, fear not. That which is about you at present settles into harmonious tranquillity and joy. All fear shall be driven out. Remember always, that where there is light, there is dark, and in the darkest moment, there is light.

Dear one, all is well, all is as it must be, we each walk our path of choice, and for some they maketh of the way, difficult. Yet, no one walks their way alone, we walk always as with the One, and walking in the light and harmony of the One. No thing, no one, goes unannounced upon their path, though at times they feel so.

Joy, is but a whisper, a breath from and in each being, we need but realise we are the joy. We bring joy to the self and to others, as do they in turn bring joy to each other. For in *fulfilling* the self we *fulfil* those about us. So too, in sadness we reach out to others, but in this, so many turn aside and do not fulfil the needs of self, and others alike. For is not one the balance and evenness of the other? You, child, have tasted deeply of both and know and *feel* the way of both.

Thus, you may help and reach out to many. Those who dip deeply in, to all that they are and maybe, shall dip deeply into life. Living each day, in truth of being. Living each moment, in line with all that is. Go ahead, pick up your bundle

and look about, to those you may help upon your way. And
know, in the passing we each help one another. Know, that
the knowing is the reward, and the knowing lasts always.

Vibrations

Child of light and beauty, that which seems difficult passes, but look back just a little way and note the lesson. There is no shame in asking for help, just as we help so let others help. Then in times of need, it is but recognition of one and another's space and necessity.

Thus, walking gently we recognise and see all that is about us. We may also feel and sense, the energies and vibrations of all that is about us. Then in this, we strengthen the awareness of self also, for we need to attune to the self and its needs, energies and vibrations. Do not neglect the necessities of the self. Lessons may be internal, as well as external, and the forces are no less effective and essential, and of no lesser importance. Often, we believed, that what is external to the self, can and does reflect all that we may or should be. Therefore, under estimating our greatest teacher the *Self*. For if we listen to, and take note of the senses of self more often, we would walk less in troubled shoes.

This does not mean, that we turn in on the notion of self-glory, and manifest unto and only that which 'I believe I am'. It means only, that we are aware of the notion of self, and that in the awareness, this self may be a teacher and is a teacher, worthy *also* of note.

Ask others! Ask self! *Then trust* and act upon that which

you know to be truth and wisdom. It becomes clearer now, in your struggles with self-lessons, for now is your time to blossom into beauty. Then, in this state, you shall touch many. Many now awaken and blossom forth upon the morning of growth and beauty. This time is powerful, and full of the power of beauty and love. It is a time, where many shall wonder at their *slow* awakening, to all this beauty about them. They shall wonder why they have been blind, for side tracking is a universal tool, that once recognised loses power. It is time, to *go* ahead in beauty, and in love of self. Self-recognition, is recognition of all that is. Yet, use the recognition and the power that comes with it, wisely. Do harm, to no other.

Go, in peace and light, to experience the beauty.

Explore The Wisdom

Child of light and of love, we greet thee, and in all that is, we bend to thee, as thee to others. Wave gently in the breeze, tall and slender, that all obstacles may melt away and blow by without restraint. Hold not, that which is not yours to hold. We may reach out to others in trouble or distress, but we may not take their bundle from them, yet, for a moment we may ease it, and them, a little. However, it is not ours to remove. For in the removal regardless of intention, we may deprive the person of an important lesson.

As the sun rises, so from darkness comes light. This light belongs to all and is the gift of new beginnings. Leave behind each day that which is no longer needed or relevant, and move ahead refreshed and free of burdens. Knowing, that the sense of burden may be self-inflicted. Quite often, we burden the self with unnecessary cares and woes, shake the self and start afresh with the dawn.

Let the past lie, in its place. Know that, what may be needed from the past region will come to the fore of its own volition, when and if required. We do not need, to dwell in this place, for our true time is in the now, and is of, the now.

Look back only in wisdom, to view the past as it was, then look now in wisdom, to what is. And then, living this moment, we may look ahead in wisdom creating the future; as does the light create the new day, by moving or appearing to move back, the darkness.

The magic of illusion lightens the heart, and brings joy to the soul. Remember the wonder of magic, as experienced by the child you were, and still are. The magic of life, is all about thee. Go into the new day and explore the magic of illusion, for behind it lies the beauty and wonder of truth.

Go, explore the day in all its glory. Go, with peace and love in your heart and mind, and on your tongue.

The Power Of Peace

As ever, dear one, we await thee. In service and in love, we stand with thee in all things and at all times. We gather to speak as one for the many. We gather to speak of love and of harmony. Harmony with and of those, and of that which is near and afar. For in the harmony of all things, there can be nought but love, and in true love of all there is, there can be peace.

A peace so profound, that every particle of life shall be drawn into the peace of all that is. Thus, all beings shall be in harmony with one another, and in this harmony of life all shall be as it should, and that which has been damaged and forsaken shall again be. Being as one with all.

The peace that is in and around the beings in the mist of time, now and past is yours to share with all who attend here. All who gather in the name of light and love, share in this peace, and shall go ahead and share this essence of life with all, in whom they contact, even as in passing. For the power of peace grows stronger, and it shall not be avoided, nor in times ahead, ignored.

No longer, shall we brush aside the gifts that are offered, for they in themselves have grown in power and in urgency. The energy of peace, manifests in all things at this time and all shall take note and act, for they shall have no choice but to take part in the surge of peace and love, and in these, harmony shall follow and pervade all that is upon this plane.

Those who fear, may fall away, yet, they shall be held up by those who have courage and thus, all shall come to the knowing in the time that is now upon us all.

This is a time of true rejoicing and in the revelry many shall gather and in the gathering, draw to the selves the wisdom of ages, for once again it is at hand and we have but to be, and in being to become part with and of the wisdom of the All.

Fear not, dear one, understanding is within and it comes to the conscious surface in time, and indeed as and when needed. You have in the past experienced this depth of understanding, and shall again know and experience the understanding that links all life, in all forms. That, which now seems unattainable and strange, shall once again be made clear and in a way, as to forbid denial of any kind and of any form.

Know we walk with thee in peace and light, and in the harmony and way of the All, with and in all life. Amen.

Replenish

Dear friends, good morning.

Greetings, child. The inner energies and powers are refreshed and strengthened in the silence of, and stillness of being. Find this place within and draw what is needed to the self, replenish the particles of the being that need restoration, and in the act fret not, that there may be this need. Remember, no one is isolated and alone, we are each and all part of the One and of the other, and as beings of life we need refreshing, and restoring, on occasion.

Now is the time, to put the energies of self in order. And this, and many other tasks require focus and strength, not only of will but also of the physical being. Take time to recoup that which is yours, thus in time you and the others will have the tools of wisdom to go forth in strength of being, and in the strength of a force of beings, to right the wrongs.

This may seem a fearsome and giant task but all is prepared and each has only to be, as of the self in truth, light, love and peace. And in the sincerity and serenity of being, they too, shall find all that lies within true peace. Bringing to those who seek, the serenity of being. Then, in this peace, a truth and calmness in the knowledge *of all* life, shall embrace all. Each shall be amazed, by the clarity of living and the wisdom held in the mere particles of life around all and in all. For they, shall then be open to all that surrounds and fills, each and every moment of their day.

Such awakening to the wisdom of all shall bring joy and glory to the many, and they shall wonder at their slow progress to this point in time. Yet, nothing is wasted, nor should be regretted, for the journey was needed and is part of the awakening.

What was lost, is once again found and may be recovered for the greater good of all. Do not neglect, nor abuse that which is found, nor use it against another. It is for the greater glory of all, and each shall take their part as decreed, or they may sit in veiled ignorance of all that is about them. Those who take up the challenge, need to look also to that which may seem insignificant, for it may indeed, be the greater part of that which is, of the whole.

Every sense of the being, is called to account and to participate, neglect no one part of the self, nor the aspects of life that that part of the self acknowledges. It is necessary, to be in tune and whole, take time to balance the self, and all of the self's parts, bringing together a perfect being of light and love. One that may work, in unison with the All Mighty, now and at all times.

Go, in light and love - always and ever - knowing, you walk, not alone.

Thank you.

Baptism

Child, we speak with you in so many ways. Humankind is stepping into the abyss of truth, and finally they take this step willingly, in trust and love.

For too long, they have hesitated, yet, even in this hesitation there has been growth and development, and newness of self. Each individual has come to this point, as of a new beginning and shall go from here, bathed in beauty of mind and spirit.

It is, as of a baptism, but this is of personal choice. No other chooses this path for the initiate, they each come of the self, and have taken the choice in both hands, and of open and clear mind. Thus the way ahead shall seem as of a path bathed in clarity and beauty, and that which is beheld upon the journey shall be of a beauty yet unperceived of the conscious mind. Know though, that the unconscious is fully aware, and awaits the unison of both.

In the unison, of that which is perceived and that which is unperceived, there is the power of self, and of all things that one feels, is lacking in their day and in their life. Know that, this information and wisdom has in all things been at hand, and in times of desire or need, we have often reached into this abyss and drawn forth our desired truth, power, or knowing.

Do not, misuse the wisdom, that now is at hand.

Go in peace and love, and know thy way. Acknowledging the all within and without. And in all things come to and join with the *One* in all. Amen.

Nature

Dear friends, thank you for the creatures who visit me, and for the feather at my door.

Child that which you are about, takes shape in many things. It is, that you need to take heed of all that comes your way. At first, you may not know the message, but take heed and in no time at all, the message shall become clear. Stoop, even to retrieve the smallest rock that calls to you, and gradually you will see the picture form.

Set aside a space in your mind, and in your heart, that the development of such a picture may easily take shape. Do not try to mould it, allow it to form of itself. Then, much that has seemed hidden, shall again appear before thee. For thy gratification and use.

Remember, when using such wise medicine to use it well, honouring those that have gifted you with their knowing. In all walk in and with love.

It is time, to shed that which you no longer need. Time, to move on lighter and less burdened. Time, to stand for all that you are. Time, to be about the business, for which you are prepared.

You walk in light, and shall do so always. You walk with the many, and have done so from time immemorial. And in thus, it is time to open and reach out to those about you, who seek the way of light and love.

Rhythm Of Life

Good morning.

And to you, child, it is a glorious morning. And the glory of the All, is in all. We await and awaken to the dawning in one and all, as does the sun to each new day.

There is movement afoot and it flows gently with and around many. They shall be caught up and moved gently with the flow, as a loving mother catches up her child and gently cradles it to her breast, to love and protect.

The movement heralds a new period of time and growth for many. It heralds a period of beauty and joy, a time of opening the heart, and the *all* of our aspect, to the song of life. Move with the rhythm of joy, and live life to the full.

Each of us, has the power and the gift of true life within, and we need to once again move to the rhythm of life. Move with it, not against and thus, to flow in harmony with all others. And with all of those who appear invisible, yet, are about our every moment, and our every pace.

All life upon and about this earth, is sacred in being, as are each of my children, and no one of these goes un-tended.

Walk in peace, walk gently upon thy mother, knowing she loves and nurtures all her children. No one is more, nor less than another, and in each day open wide thy arms and heart to those about thee.

Re-Charge

Dear child, look about you at the beauty. Look to the depth, for beauty hidden from view. Know often that the surface may be a disguise, or may disguise that which emerges unsolicited and often unattended, just as a bud pushes up through the ground, seemingly unaided, and certainly in the main unnoticed. First the ground seems bare then fertile, so too, those about us and the scene about us, may seem bare and infertile. However, with love and nurturing, even so, a desert may bloom into untold beauty. Yet, remember, the beauty was always there. It needs but to be, perceived so.

Now today, gather the energy about you, to you. Re-charge the self and share this energy, with the mother and with those about you. They in turn, will thus share and learn of the ways of sharing with self and with others. To share with self, is to honour the being you are, and in so honouring the self, we may honour all our relations.

Let not the smallest of these slip from our grasp unattended, and know that only a thought may be required. Often we believe it is their deeds that we do that are most important, yet, likewise the thought, is of importance and indeed, may be all that is required.

Both deed and thought share in importance, yet, neither is of value if the intent is unworthy. Know, the intent is known and in deceiving others, we deceive only the self. Be aware of intent, in all *works* that are done, or offered for another. If they cannot be supported by *true* intent, they are best left, undone.

In humility, be about your day.

Time

Dear friends it is sometime since I have sat to write.

Child of light, all is well with thee. It is but time, and in time, all things are held in place. Yet, time maybe an illusion. It is how we use it, that is relevant or not.

We are at hand, in all things and at all times. Walk softly, in thy ways and fear not thy destiny. We are near and draw nearer, day by day. Things again move forward, the time of rest recedes again into the day, and the time of action and knowing step forward, into the light of day. Be, thy self and make note of thy knowing. For in so doing, all may have access to the will of the way, the Light of lights.

Many, as yourself, shall open the way for so many more, that all may have the opportunity to walk the way of light and love.

Go in peace, go in light, and know we welcome your presence in all things. Walk softly upon the way child and know we walk ever with thee in all that you do.

Thank you.

Coming And Going

Child, it is with delight that we greet thee, and those about thee at this time. Note, the comings and goings at present and record what you perceive. For there is much afoot and we ask thy help in the spreading of joyous tidings.

Those near to you who at this time are troubled, shall have the pain eased, in that they shall be shown a way of moving forward and in the movement thus the pain shall ease away. It is not of your making, know this and hold to the joy of their release.

Much shall come your way and you shall again see the way ahead clear. You have been in a period of intense learning, much as yet you have been unaware of, but the time of movement now cannot be denied.

Watch for and note, the changes about you, they shall be quite clear; you need not search them out, just be alert and watch as things unfold in unison, right before thee. Do all things in and with gentleness and love. Then fear not, all else.

Go in peace child, for there is enough here at present. Note, that from this time now, you may be awakened to knowing and knowledge, write it forth with, that it may be retained and utilised as needs be.

Be not afraid of that which presents itself, for the enquirer shall come for the knowledge and wisdom held here.

And thus it shall be, as if dispensed.

Amen, I say to thee. Amen to all and to the All in all things. Go now, and step gently upon thy way.

Remember

Dear friends, please help me settle today, draw near and place your love about me.

Child, in all, we are ever with you. Gentleness be your way and mode of thought and deed. All goes well and is as it should be. Remember, in all things we walk with you and by you.

Hold fast to your way and your purpose shall be clear to you and to all about you. We are each responsible for our own deeds and actions, and thoughts, no other is responsible for the self. Be at peace with the self, and know you do your best in all things.

Trust in the self, for you have come a long way in your growth and wisdom. Do not turn now from all that is at hand, instead reach out in faith and trust, and take hold of that which you have created, that which you shall share with many. Look about still, and be prepared to learn from those, and that which is about you.

Open the eyes, the mind and the heart, to all who would reach out to you in wisdom and love, to share what they have with thee.

Go now, about your day in peace and harmony, and walk gently upon thy way.

Thank you.

Oneness

Yes child, we are with you, is the day not beautiful. Even in this plateau of colour, there are many shades of blue, white, grey and green. Each a force on its own and re-enforcing its neighbours strength. The light of the morning touches each and enriches it with light, warmth and power. The power of regeneration and life.

The earth below, and the sky above blend to conceal the start and end of each, forming oneness and wholeness of being. Even the craft in which you now sit, blends with the air and is supported on wings of light and energy.

In the far distance, there appears stillness and peace, yet, no thing stands still. For in all life, there is continuous movement and growth. And in this a growth of spirit, yet, untold, unfelt and unknown to the lay being, or uninitiated. Yet, now there are processes in practice to rectify and re-verse this appearance of ignorance, for no one is in total ignorance, just in various states of re-awakening.

Note, all that comes thy way, and be of open mind and heart. The future unfolds gently, as you go *gently* upon the way. Look now for the words of wisdom, and trust in the knowing they shall bring. We cannot give of falsehood, but of truth alone, we share with thee and thou. Know in thy heart all is well, and that light and love shine forth upon thee, and from thee.

Walk in peace and joy, as you go gently upon the way.

Thank you.

Feel The Words

Good morning dear friends, would you please share your wisdom with me, and guide my steps through each day.

Child of light and wonder, it is good to share a moment with you, and in this special moment there is much to share and pass on, just as you shall also pass on, what you learn. Fear not, that you sometimes feel the words escape you, sit quietly and when the time is right the words shall flow as a river unleashed. And child, you will know the time, for it now draws near, as does the beauty of being whole with the All.

Many strive for wholeness of being some too hard, others in a manner not worthy of such little effort, yet, all is known, and each effort in truth or in false pretence, are known and audited.

Take care, and note that which comes thy way, and in truth and love act upon the knowing that is unleashed from within, for now you come in to a state of a ripened being, and the fruit that you are, shall feed the souls of many. Do not doubt these words. It is that which is within that ripens, and is ready for the picking or offering, to those that come. Offer freely, and with love of self and of other. Those that need to pick from thy tree shall be guided, you need but loose the chosen fruit to their care. Know, that in all things you are replenished, guarded and truly loved. Be at peace with the self, child, and also with those about thee, sending always thoughts of love.

The weights fall lightly from thee, as if unnoticed and you step gracefully and gently upon thy way in all things. There is magic about thee. In all things, see the beauty and the magic of being the self, as you are and as you are intended to be, step upon your way with head held high and with feet gently touching the path, so as not to damage or harm that which may, for a brief moment, be under foot. Look even to the smallest, that ye may learn its ways, and know thine own.

Go in love and peace, in all that you do and know the answers come near, that you and others may learn. Your journey, has been and ever shall be fruitful. Share thy fruits, yet, waste not of the fruit, and pick up and cherish that which falls, until the one that needs it, comes. Then, with loving heart give it freely to the caller, for it is theirs to have and taste of, and in thus fill the need they have.

In seeking outward, many shall come to know the inner wisdom, and shall find peace and joy, in being of and with the self in all things, coming to the remembrance of the Almighty presence, that is within and all around each one of us,

Go in peace, about the day.

Thank you.

Ask The Way

Yes, child, we await and would speak with you. Today, we start anew with wonders to unfold.

There is much speculation and scepticism in the world today, but hold to truth, and trust the inner knowing that unfolds in thee. Each has a place and a time in which to serve, and there are many that shall serve, each in their own quiet and personable way. No one, is less nor more than the other, and each has their place.

Once again, we tell you that many gather, here upon this land and in many others. Each holds a key to a part, and each has a role to exercise. The joining of many brings peace and harmony to the whole, and in their strength and love of all things, so rests the harmony of the ages, and thus within this state, the wisdom of the way.

And the way is ahead, all around and within. And in this, there is balance, light and true wisdom. Wisdom gentle and pure of nature, awaits all who would sup of it, and there is enough for all, if they would but ask the way, to the All That Is.

Know my children, that this way is not difficult, it lies below the feet if you but look. Open your eyes and your heart, and ask in truth and trust to be shown the way. It is not a difficult and entangled way, but one of beauty, love and joy and all may walk it. There is, but need only to cleanse the mind and heart, and to lessen the load you carry.

Children of light and love, raise up the eyes now, and trust the feet to tread smoothly the path you walk. For it is guarded by the true thoughts of many, that have gone ahead in joyful wonderment. Each of you too may experience this joy, if you but trust the self and all that is about you.

Remember, the purity of mind and heart that a child has, and that you have safely locked within, go now and unlock the treasures you have saved, for *now* is the time to open your precious treasurer chest. Open it gently and with love, and visit each gift in turn, re- connecting and re-acquainting the self, with the self of long ago, yet, of now.

Then in your oneness of self, you are whole and may be about your way, doing as intended, as prepared. For this, you have chosen to be. Walk then in love and light, and know your way, for you have mapped the course and have the map, safely upon your person.

Amen, I say to you, follow your way in truth. Step gently along the path, and hold the seed of trust safely to the heart. Let the mind dwell on the now, lighting all that is about you and draw on the wisdoms that unfold, savouring the needs of self and those who gather thus to walk in harmony and peaceful desire.

My children, walk gently upon the way and gather that which inspires and delights. Holding these gifts as treasures of thought and deed, to the self within, and knowing that each treasure enriches all that you are, and all that is.

Amen, I say, go now about your way, walk in peace and light always. Just as we walk always, with thee.

Joy of Joys

Greetings, as ever we stand ready. The time between makes, no difference, as to us, it is of nothing – no time at all.

Dear child, let go of the confusion and hold fast to thy trust in the All. That which is, is. Know, that all proceeds as need be in the overall plan of things. That which shall be is near to hand, and it goes well with thee.

Joy of joys, the morning breaks clear and fresh, a new day, a new start. Let each new dawn shower beauty and joy, upon the situations that may arise with the sun. All that is new and fresh is beauty personified. Allow the beauty and joy to flow all about thee, in all that you do and think, let each new situation be an adventure into the wonders, that abound about and within thee.

Struggle not, to reach the end of the day, before it has truly begun. Take, but one moment at a time, that each may be cherished for it wonders. Thus, taking from each the strength and vitality offered. Go in joy and love, to greet the day ahead and enjoy each morsel, as it is offered thee.

Go gently, child, upon thy way, knowing the path is lined with feather down, that you may pass unheeded and unobstructed.

Thus, as you step forward this day, lift up thy head, lift up thy heart, and know all is well with thee and thou.

A blessing, child. Walk in peace. Amen.

Venture Forth

Good morning dear friends, walk with me today and always.

Good morning, child. The path lies ahead in glorious splendour, for all who would pass by and take note. There are beauties, yet unfolding, to behold. Often we question, where we should just accept and be evermore blessed.

Yet, in man, to question is both a failing and a blessing, for to question is good, to know when is sublime. Thus then, the failure to act upon the moment is to waste all that was made available.

To venture forth into the wisdom and wonder, is to venture into life itself. Do not hold back from the journey of life, in fear. For it is this fear, that sucks out the very opportunities, that the mystery of living life to the full, presents to one.

We each, have a duty to explore this life we have been given, or chosen. Yet, the very exploration of being becomes a difficult chore, if we so allow. Take up the challenge, and go forth and live each moment to its full extent.

Yet, harm neither the self, nor any other in the quest of living. No, these are not contradiction, just good sense if we value the self and all else. Life, is a treasured book of wisdom, and we may dip into any page at any time in search of learning, and of the wonders, yet, unexplored.

Learn from the wonders of life, and hold these in true regard, that we may in truth, render the wisdom gained to the beholder.

Go in wonder, and explore the day.

Thank you.

Recollections

It is joy, to speak with thee, child. That you may know and sense the way of things.

We are in thee and all that thou art, as you are in each of us. This is the way of all things in life, and know that life is a far greater landscape, than the mind may perceive of. And know also, child, that there are wonders, yet, that thou shalt perceive, and in due course new wonders will befall, upon thy path.

Remember, at this time the glorious recollections of times long past, and honour thy God in all creation. Trust in the future, that is within the living now.

Treasure the recollections, yet, harbour none that they may float freely upon the sea of life and movement. In thus, you are free also to live life and to experience, all that you desire. And in freedom, knowledge and growth of spirit, dwell. Then, in safety and love, we may know the self and all those about us.

Go, in peace.

Gifts Within

December 31st

Dear friends, on this the last day of the year will you speak with me?

Yes, child, we are ever here and would speak this day of peace and love, which abounds within and about all, who would but still the self, and know these gifts.

Know, these gifts are within you and you, and you, and that each of you, has the gift of sharing the joys of peace and love, with all others who may enter your day. These are not difficult gifts to share, each need only to reach out in truth and trust, and give openly of the self.

Know, that there is no need of restraint at this time, many need these gifts to ward off the fears they feel and harbour, at the close of your year. Yet, in all things, it is a wondrous period, in the cycle. Ending gives way to beginning, and so life proceeds as it is meant to. And without fear, peace and love welcome the new dawn, as powers of joy and fulfilment, that all may rejoice in the changeover.

Each individual, may take stock at this time and let go of that which has ended. Hold and nurture, only the new life that is emerging and taking form.

The day or period, marks the time of ending, yet, the process has been in place for some time since. No, thing starts or ends on the instant, each has a process of being.

And that process takes time, even if unattended or unnoticed. Often because we are not still, we miss the process and acknowledge the consequences. Each must therefore learn to watch for the small, seemingly insignificant moments of process, and take joy in the peace and love of life that abounds in each moment.

Amen, I say, go in peace and love, and share thy gifts.

Thank you.

New Beginnings

Yes child, it is indeed a new morning and a period of welcome, to one and all. This is a time of renewal and replenishment a time of going within and accounting. It is endings and new beginnings, a time not to be feared, but to be enjoyed. It is a time to share, and to review various encounters and events. Then a time of letting go, so as to reach out to the new, that which is yet unborn, but newly perceived of.

There is so much to share, at this time. Notions of joy and wonder, of birth, death and of re-birth. In all we rejoice and sing forth praise, and the love of all life is revered and held fast. Amen, we say to thee, open thy heart and mind, and give blessing to all that abounds thee.

Give of thy love, to those who seek it in truth and freedom, that they then, may offer love to others in truth and freedom. Love is not a bond, it is a gift, one which circles ever outward encompassing all who have need, and those who *just are,* one with self and all things.

Child, we gather with thee and about thee, and shall walk the road at thy side. Know we are ever with thee, and that it is as ordained. We walk in love and faith, and know thy courage, strength and beauty of life, as being whole.

Again, we say, do not wonder at these things for it is writ and shall be. Keep thy faith wrapped warmly about thee. In this then, you show example to those who walk thy path and pass by thee. They then, to others upon their way, and so on and so forth, as life circles outward and ever onward, as ordained.

Go with love and faith, to walk gently the day.

The Picture

Hello my friends, forgive my tardiness in not writing. I have been distracted and need help through the present maze.

Dear child, as you see the clouds before you rolling in, you know they pass on the wind, so too, you're 'perceived' troubles roll in and shall also pass. This is, but a slight hiccup, rest and roll with it; as the river goes with the flow, so too, go with the flow. It is gentle, and you need not fear the eddies, there are none. In fact child, look about as you move with the flow, and see what is about you. However, look only, do not engage at this time with side issues, stay focused on the picture before you, that which you by hard effort, have created.

Indeed, look well at the picture, for it is a masterpiece of love and devotion, and as such, shall be recognized in time. In due course, you shall be recognized as the master of this creation.

Gentle spirit, the time you now spend in this place is precious, and you shall know and appreciate this, yet, time spent elsewhere is also precious to you, and the many. Remember, each in its place and in its own time, although it sometimes seems difficult to separate the issues at hand, let time be the judge. Time mends all things. Give unto the self that you may then and only then, give unto others.

Go in peace, child, we watch over thee and thou.

Light And Love

Dear child, gentle one, we are ever at your side and the blessings of the day, are many. Walk throughout this day and those to come, with your head held high. Know, that what comes your way has been well deserved, and the gifts and joys are many.

That, which in true intent, you have asked for, shall manifest. Yet, know that, here and there, a door closes, and then in turn others open. Some, at this time, struggle with their own demons, but they shall come through the period of trial. Join with us, in charging them with light and love that their struggles may ease.

To all I say, come unto the One and lay thy troubles at the feet of Glory. That they may be lifted from thy shoulders, for we are not meant to carry such burdens alone.

If they may accept these words and lay down their woes, so the burdens may be lifted. Yet, many carry on, in a way of self-damnation and refuse to set aside that which they abhor.

** *** **

Now child, some words for the day and the time, which you are in.

Beauty and joy shall win out, and are the right not the privilege of all beings in life and light. Why do we not acknowledge our rights? Instead, we persist in the struggle and pursuit of that which is in fact, at hand.

We refuse to see, that which is before us. We go around it, over it and ignore it. Is beauty and joy, that, which we fear? Yet, they are the gifts we most desire, beauty of life and joy of living. Yet, we do fear life, and the living of it fully.

No - take hold of life, live it and *be*. Be of the self, as was meant to be, and be one with all, in all things.

Walk in peace, gentle spirit. We walk ever with thee and thou, thy kin.

Thank you

Future, The Now

Yes, child, we greet the morning with thee in all its glory. We welcome thy company and presence of mind.

This day, shall be filled with joy and love and light, as shall be many more. You and those about you may revel in the oneness of being in the now, for in the now is where presence of mind and spirit truly exist, and from this moment, we create our future way.

Let all that has passed, pass on by and create now in the present that which you desire in the future, knowing that each moment of creation, is in the *now*.

Basically, that which you do, feel and think *now*, is what you become as you move ahead, therefore a positive perspective now, creates a positive perspective in the future, and this has the power and the force, to influence many about us.

So too, the opposite – for every act has a reaction, but we may create beauty and joy, as easily as fear and tempest. Love and light, as darkness and sorrow. Go about the now, in gentleness and light, and fill each moment, thought and action, with love and joy.

Amen.

Absorb

As I work, please walk with me.

Child of light, we are ever with you in all that you are, and in all that, you do. Today is a joyous day and if seen as such, brings great rewards, to all who fully encounter the day.

Go, into the day wide eyed and open minded, reaching outward to the wisdoms collected about you. We learn not only by sight and sound, but also, by observation. Absorb all the energy that abounds about you, over the next few days, remembering there is no harm in these energies only learning experiences.

At this time, you are where you are meant to be and you have much to gain, and much to give to the present circumstances. Keeping in mind the energy and presence of the now, walk gently ahead into the day, that this day and the days ahead may be truly filled with joy and wondrous deeds, adventures and travel like you have never before experienced. Travel both of the physical being and of the spirit being within.

We walk with thee, this day and ever.

Thank you.

Open The Senses

Dear one, we are an ever open link of communication. This next period of time, is a time of advanced learning and of knowing, wisdom. Note, all that comes thy way. And in all thy senses, be receptive.

This is an exciting period that you now enter, know that you are in yourself, prepared. Many will come to teach and to learn, and the ways of learning shall be varied in all their aspects. Do not be surprised by the ideas that shall flow forth, and remember to record thy progress.

There is newness about, take note of the adventure and the journey, or passage of learning. Note also, the different directions that may be explored to wisdom. Learning is not only, of books.

Remember, the links of a chain; they are but a continuance of the other. There are many links and they are solid in their resolve. Note also the chain is open, not binding. It holds no one captive.

Peace and light, be with you always.

Thank you

What Can I Do?

Dearest child, we are ever with you. We walk by your side in all things, and know thy way is clear and safe. Do not take note of the negativity that may seem to be about you at this time, for it revolves about petty jealousy. It is not your way, nor your task to resolve it.

Now child, we are about the mammoth task of drawing together energies of the first instance. Those that have tasks to perform, are now gathered in the place of need and their work begins. The work is that of love, of sharing a love most beautiful and lasting. Of being, love most beautiful and lasting. Of knowing love most beautiful and lasting.

Now, is a time of joy, a time of being one with all that is, and of sharing in the knowing of the One, that is the All in each and every living being.

As one being, what can I do? This is so often asked or mooted, yet, there is so much that each one can and does do. Just, being as we are, and giving off the love and joy we know and trust, throws out such a ray, an energy of love and light, that is transmitted to all who may be in need and are, or perhaps are not, open to receive at this time. Yet, know this, love and beauty is not lost upon the way, for it is stored and waits only for someone to seek out, reach in, and fill their need, their desire, their longing and their day, with all that is theirs to receive.

Too often, we neglect to seek for the self. Too often, we are taught and teach, that to seek of the self is not right or proper. If it is of another's then this is so, but if it is ours to seek, then go ahead, and reach out the heart and the hand, and your desires and needs shall be met with love and joy.

Take of the fruit, that hangs freely and enjoy its wonders. Why grow upon the tree, if no one sups of the energy that lies hidden within? Is it not wasteful, to allow the fruit to fall ignored and neglected from the vine of life? Let life be fulfilled and fruitful. Share that which you have, with those about thee, the wisdom, joy and beauty that they may, know and share *love,* with all in whom they encompass.

Trust, child in thy own love and inner beauty, and be about thy task in good and faithful spirit, for you are never alone and your way is prepared and clear of stones. That which you need to impart, is here within, just open the heart and reach out the hand, knowing that the work you are about, is right for the moment, and in the moment right and proper for those who come to learn.

Go in peace and light, enjoy the days ahead for they are many, and they are fruitful for the self and many others about thee.

Unto thee, in joy and love. Amen.

Be Mindful

Dear one, it is with delight and pleasure that we welcome thee this night. There is much noise and disturbance about thee, but it is not for you to worry the self. We must all deal with our own situations. It is well that you are rested, and once again in balance with self and with nature about thee.

As you have rightly supposed, often a message for one may also apply to another. Note, often in thy work, a word or two for the self. If it feels so, then it is so. Be guided by thy feelings. Trust the feelings and the inner knowing, and be ever true to the self at all times. Often we are confused by the messages we receive, but know and be guide by the self.

You have things to learn, one from the other, and each from the All. Be open and mindful of that which is there to be shared and to be learned, so as to share and teach to others in the times ahead.

You have respect, and shall give and get respect from those in whose company you may sit. The sitting in, of circles generates an inner energy, and also an earth energy from which you do, and may draw on, to your hearts ease and contentment. From these meetings and gatherings, you shall grow in wisdom and in light energy, so as to go forth from here, prepared, when the time comes.

There is no need of fear as you walk into the future, now

and in the times ahead. Many forget, that the future is the now, as is the past, for each clings one to the other, to create all that is, and all that may be.

Yet, do not rush ahead, let the pleasure of learning and knowing, unfold gracefully and gently upon thy being. Take time, in thy schedule, for the self. Remembering, time is a flexible, elastic commodity that we may use to our own ends. All that is required, shall be met.

Rest now, and look upon the morrow with wonder and delight..

Serenity

Yes, child, as always we are here with you. We know and feel the anxiety that at times overwhelms thee. Yet, too we know and see thy strength and beauty of spirit, know this strength and beauty is of the physical self also.

It is a calmness that pervades the space about thee, and that draws others to this space. Yet, you argue what calmness? Know, child, it is there and you do exude this quality of spirit. Many are drawn to you and to the atmosphere about you. Trust, it is there and will again arise to your awareness, in due course.

There have been great leaps of wisdom upon this way, and though you doubt the self at times, all is well with thee and thou.

Soon, that which is awaited, will enter upon thy way and there shall be no sudden surprise, only beauty and joy of the utmost purity, both of spirit and soul.

Look to the star, and know thy way upon the earth, for there is again movement ahead of thee, there is no need of wonder at this time, for it is the heart's desire and we know it.

Come child, rejoice in thy way, and give love and pleasure where you may. Know too, that love of self is a great gift to offer others. For in this, they learn love of self.

The purpose about you at present is to give freely of the

self, do not constrain the true self, as it is that which is needed now in this place. Give of love and beauty, give of joy and wonder. Share the child within qualities, with these, the people about thee. I know of these people, they know of me. And through those, such as you, we may again be reunited in the One in all things.

Go now, child, and rest, as we restore thy strength in sleep. Amen

Ho

Good morning, we rejoice at your coming to this place. Now, we may write the words to share with all about thee. And dear one, there are indeed many to write.

Now slipping sideways, we begin.

Ho! We greet each and all who visit this space, and time in space. Many gather now, to share their accumulated wisdoms with those who would listen and read here in. Know, that that which is shared, comes only in truth for we are bound in truth, and can act only from the perspective, of this realm.

Many now gather and know the way of things and of their way in time, yet, they too heed and desire support and reassurance in their task, and daily comings and goings.

Much shall and will be henceforth shared upon these pages, and also in meetings and gatherings of like-minded individuals. Know, that by example and practice many shall come also to enquire of those of like mind. The wisdom of ages now pushes forth, and up from the depths of past times, to reach out and forth, to all who wish to know and learn these truths.

Yet, in knowing, one cannot stand still and let it by, for in reaching out and supping, you have thus made the commitment to truth and light. The work thereof, does not sit still upon the heart. It works and desires to work, with one

and all that shall come this way. And gladden the heart and
soul, shall this wisdom, with joy. For this is one of the responsibilities of truth and love, to gladden, not burden. No
one who chooses this way shall be burdened.

And unto them shall spring such joys as yet unperceived
of in this their presence upon this way and time.

Awakenings shall now begin to unfold and in quantities
that as to make one feel to burst, though they shall not, but
burst out with joy and wonder to all, who may perceive of
them. This quality of truth and love shall glow forth for all
to perceive of and know. Such shall be the wonders, and
the wonderings of all who *see*. And such shall be, the knowing and learning in unison with one and all who visit here,
this space and time. They shall know. They shall come. And
then, this work of truth and joy shall flow, as of the river of
life, to all who sup.

Know, that each one now hears and feels the call to wisdom and truth. Thus, onto love, joy and beauty of spirit
and being.

Go now in peace. We shall speak again, as the awakenings unfold upon thy way.

There Is Time

Dear child, we are ever present and walk and talk with thee often in spirit ways. All that is, is and is as it is meant to be at this time, have no fear or dread of the steps that be ahead of thee. That, which is now in place flows to the heart, soul and spirit of times ahead.

Many now move in meeting places, forming circles of wisdom and learning. These places are many and varied, yet, of one knowing and sharing. That which draws many, is the desire of knowing, yet, forgets not that which is innate and known. It is a time now of unlocking, recalling and facing full ahead, of recognizing and accepting, that which in each, is a treasure to be shared once again, with all who desire to sup.

Come in joy and love to the work. Those that now walk this way, have much to do in the companionship of others. Yet, often seemingly alone and unnoticed.

Recall again, no thing goes unnoticed or unattended, nor does any one being, go unnoticed, unattended. Whichever way be chosen, no one goes alone upon their way.

There is much to do, yet, preparation has been done, each preparing in their own way and in their own time for the march upon the wisdoms of old. Even as to the ancients, much is in progress for the way now is clear of static and turbulence. The airways so to speak are clear and those who would be still and listen, will and shall hear the words of old and of the now, for each is of the one and of the other, in all that is and shall be.

Do not query that which seems entangled, for it is not. In depths, each knows of the way to understanding, to peace of mind and spirit. There is velvet upon the path, smooth and luxurious in texture, touch and knowing. So walk forth, bare foot and trusting, look up and ahead, knowing the safety and security of each footfall. Knowing and recognizing the wisdom of each dew drop upon the brow. Knowing and being of the self in all about thee. Recognizing the self and its place in all that is, and all that abounds in this time and place.

Gather up now each one of you all that you require, for the journey ahead is long and varied and the work ahead is joyous. The wonders ahead are plentiful and bounteous and the knowing is glorious and rewarding in its simplicity of spirit and being.

Jump not from one to another, but take time to be and to absorb the being of self, of now and of all that abounds about thee. And each, to the self be true and faithful in living, and in spirit of being natural, of self and of wisdom.

The wisdom of ages and the ancient ones, draws now to beings of light and love, all that they desire and need, they have but to reach out and ask. Asking of the self and of others, for through these each one and another, may be helped and thus grow in spirit, and grace of being part with one and all.

There is so much, yet, time is now set aside for the work to flow, as of the river of life. And as the pen moves, so shall the flow increase, and flow with and of an ease, as to inspire generations of loyalty and love, of one and all.

Bringing a time of joy, peace and light, to all who have faith in self and life, as in being of one and of The All.

Yes! Yes! It shall flow as time is given. And as one grows in peace and quiet, as you shall, there is time enough, for all that is needed to be done.

Go now, in peace and light, upon thy day of joy.

Seeds Of Joy

It is a good morning, child of light, and with the dawn of day and of time, comes enlightenment and beauty of spirit, for each and all shine forth, anew and reborn.

There is ahead a tender time of spirit. A time of rejoicing and of renewal, for the energies strengthen and spread out, as to the flow of nature. Each should work with the flow, and gather strength of purpose to the self and of the self, as to work harmoniously in the presence of the One, in the now. Work always in the spirit of all that exists and abounds, in, with and about thee. So too, each shall gather to the self, that which is needed now and in the times ahead, for there is much to be about and to be of, for the good of all that is, in being.

Safely gather the seeds of joy, that they may be scattered upon the winds of progress, indeed joyful and necessary. For in the seed, is held the secret of life eternal and ever.

If ye plant, prepare the way and sow wisely, as much is often expected, of such a small parcel of wonder. Watch then, as the joys unfold and spread forth their wonders to all, who perceive of them. Then as each is gathered forth, so they in turn may be shared, and share with the gatherers, their wonders to behold.

Such joy awaits all who gather, and all who sow.

Pulsate

Dear friends in light and love, hello.

Dear one, it is with joy we reach out and behold thee in this twilight period. We welcome your company and rejoice in your presence. Many who know thee, gather here at this time, to share in thy company and pleasure.

Know child, that which you seek is near at hand, and you shall in growth, open to many wonders and wisdoms. That which lays dormant stirs within, and readies to awaken anew to the work of light and love, and in so doing to bring these gifts and wonders, to many who await the return of wisdom and wise ways.

For, too long, the wise ways have lain dormant as in sleep, but no, there was a need of waiting. Waiting for the time, when again *all* shall come together in love and peace, to give glory to the *One* in all. This time draws near, when we shall gather together in praise and harmony, to glorify the light source within all life.

Many, gather about the earth to charge and rejuvenate the light energy hidden deep within, know that this energy pulses in harmony with all life. It rises in strength to the surface to share with all, the joy of knowing, the joy of wisdom, and the joy of pure understanding.

Fear not the words, as you grow, so too, they grow and

in time clarity shines forth for all to perceive, if they would.

Join us daily, if thou may and more shall pour forth upon the page of life. Open the mind and the heart, and it follows, the eyes shall open.

In peace. Amen.

Thank you.

Riddles

Dearest child of light, all that is at present, is well. You as others, are in a state of transition and this augers a time of flux and flow, of somewhat an irregular pattern. Yet, there is clarity of purpose and position, in the way of things, just ahead.

Try for the moment, to relax into the flow and drift this way and that with the flow. Do not fight or push against it, for all is well and the way is lighted and prepared. And shall be clearly known to thee, at the moment of contact.

Do not worry, as to the way you feel of the moment, all is well. One just restores oneself to the equal and fairly way of things. And all shall be fair and equal unto thee, here under the stars of love and light. Are they not bright and cheerful of the present time? Do they not shine on thee?

Yes.

Child of wonder, do not fret thyself all is well in thy way, and all goes as prescribed. For you have writ so, in the company of the many, and they in thy company have also writ. So shall it be, and so shall the time of gathering be as of all who predestined the way of joy and light unto all. That which was programmed, so shall it be, in the beauty of all and shall be now again at hand. Let not the time pass unattended. Be watchful and alert, for each is called to act on the will of things prepared.

The period of rest and relocation draws neigh. Then following, so too, act upon the way of love and light, in joyous and beautiful strains of voice and wisdom. That which you need is provided. You have more at hand than you presently and consciously realize and know in your every day way of being.

Thy inner being, thy self is well prepared and alert, and awaits only the signal of light and knowing, to then openly act upon the self and be of one with the All in self. Then there shall be rejoicing in this place, as yet, unknown and perhaps long since forgotten in times ancient and past, but it shall reawaken and many shall recall and remember the way of old. Yet, not old, but refreshed and seemingly new of old.

It seems we speak in riddles, yet, it is not a riddle but a pathway, that is and has been well trod.

Go, in peace and love, and fret not, thy way is clear. Amen.

Thank you

Acknowledgements

Blessings to family and friends, past and present, who have walked this path with me – patiently.

To the mediums Gwen and Marg who encouraged my development;

Catherine for her computer assistance and expertise;

Tracie for her spiritual and artistic guidance.

I am especially grateful to 'The Committee' for their continued love, guidance and wisdom, without their presence none of this would have been possible.

To all,
Thank you.

About the Author

Norma Fenttiman, an intuit of mind and senses was born in New South Wales. After the death of her father, Norma and her mother moved to Tasmania. There she met her future husband at age sixteen.

In 1970, with her husband and son, she settled in Western Australia.

Throughout these years she experienced numerous intuitive events, following in her mother's footsteps. Norma accepted these occurrences as being the normal way of things.

In her fifties she returned to university where a group of her friends persuaded her to acknowledge, and act upon, her intuitive abilities.

Desiring guidance, Norma began writing in diary form and the words began to fall upon the page.

Over a period of ten years these words and insights brought wonder and peace of mind as well as the belief and desire to share them with those about her.

www.ingramcontent.com/pod-product-compliance
Lightning Source LLC
Chambersburg PA
CBHW060941050726

47592CB00003B/1049